The Day Came True

Simon Adorian

THE CAST

 Mrs Turner
 Miss Cherry
 Zak
 Indira Das TV Presenter
 Luke Leppard TV Presenter

 Jojo
 Sunita
 Director
 Mr Green
 Mrs Green

 Sam
 Cleo
 Mouse
 Donut
 Police Officer

 Other children at Story Street Primary School
 Other members of the TV film crew
 Police Officers

Scene 1

Outside the front of Story Street Primary School. The building is decorated with banners, bunting and balloons. A big sign reads,

"Story Street Primary School – Happy 200th Birthday!"

A TV film crew is setting up a shot of Mrs Turner being interviewed by Indira Das, one of the presenters of 'Make Your Dreams Come True.' The TV Director is in charge. In the background there is a large crowd including Miss Cherry, Jojo, Sam, Sunita and Cleo.

Director Is everybody ready, then? Indira, are you ready to roll?

Indira I think we're there.

Director Can we have everybody quiet, please? Remember, we want all you kids in the back of the shot cheering and waving until I signal you to stop. Then you'll need to be completely silent for Indira's introduction. Have you got that? And … action!
The children all cheer until the Director raises an arm. All go quiet as Indira talks into a microphone.

Indira Hello and welcome to TV's favourite family show –

Children *(Shouting)* Make Your Dreams Come True!

Indira I'm Indira Das and this is the show that spreads a bit of happiness. This week's edition comes to you live from the town of Wellbridge, where we're going to meet the teachers and children of Story Street Primary School.
The children all cheer loudly.

Indira Let's start by having a word with the school's head teacher, Mrs Susan Turner.

Mrs Turner Good afternoon, Indira.

Indira Now, you've got a rather special party going on here today, haven't you?

Mrs Turner We have indeed. It's our 200th birthday party!

Indira I see. And where did you get the idea for this wonderful event?

Mrs Turner Well, it all started when I was looking back through the old school diaries and I discovered that the school was opened exactly 200 years ago this weekend.

Indira 200 years old. Now that's something worth celebrating, isn't it?

Mrs Turner Just what I thought. I talked to the children in assembly and they were just as keen as I was to make a big day of it. Weren't you, kids?
The children all cheer loudly.

Indira Let's hear from one or two of these kids now.
Director gives a signal for Jojo and Sam to step forward and join Indira.

Indira And your names are …?

Jojo Jojo Macdonald …

Sam And Sam Summerday.

Scene 1

Indira Tell us a little bit about today's special party.

Mr and Mrs Green wander in front of the camera.

Mr Green Ah, there you are, Sam.

Sam looks very embarrassed. The Director looks angry.

Sam Not now, Mr Green.

Director *(To the TV crew)* And cut it there!

Mr Green We were just wondering if anyone could tell us where we could get a nice cup of tea. The invitation did say there would be refreshments, didn't it, dear?

Mrs Green Oh yes.

Director Excuse me. Don't you two realise that you've just walked into shot? Can't you see we're trying to make a television programme here?

Mr Green There's no need to talk to me like that! This is my old school and I'll have you know that I'm a guest of honour today. Besides, all we want is a cup of tea. We're thirsty, aren't we, dear?

Mrs Green Oh yes, we'd love a nice cup of tea.

Director *(Growing angrier)* Oh for goodness' sake! Will someone please show them where they can get a drink?

Sam On the playing field round the back. There's a big tent and they're serving tea in there.

Mr Green Very kind, I'm sure.

Mrs Green We'll get out of your way now.

Director Thank you.

Exit Mr and Mrs Green.

Director All right, Indira, we'll go back to the interview with the two kids. And … action!

Indira So, Sam and Jojo. Tell us all about this special party that the school is holding.

Sam It was Mrs Turner's idea to have the party. She thought we should invite lots of people who went to this school in the past.

Indira Great idea!

Jojo So our class wrote hundreds of invitations to old pupils.

Sam Like Mr Green there. He used to go to this school in the old days.

Indira But you didn't just invite local people, did you?

Sam No, we got replies from all over the world.

Jojo One ex-pupil wrote to us from the South Pole. He's a scientist.

Sam And we got a reply from Japan.

Jojo And then Mrs Turner hired a big tent to go on the playing field. After all, it's not every day you have a 200th birthday party. And then the idea was that we could use the tent for the party and for the wedding.

Indira Ah yes, the wedding. Tell us about the wedding, Mrs Turner.

Mrs Turner Well, one of my young teachers, Miss Cherry, is engaged to be married to the well-known children's author, Zak Pieman.

Indira *The* Zak Pieman? Author of *Pieman's Rhymin' Tales?*

Mrs Turner The very same.

Scene 1

Indira I think it's time we met the lovely bride, Miss Rosie Cherry.

Miss Cherry steps forward to be interviewed. She is wearing a wedding dress.

Indira So, Rosie, tell us about these wedding plans.

Miss Cherry Well, when the school birthday party was arranged, Zak and I realised that we had already fixed our wedding date for the very same day.

Indira A clash of dates. Whatever did you do about that?

Miss Cherry We decided to keep the date and hold the wedding here today as well. We thought it would be nice to invite all the children and staff to the wedding.

Scene 1

Indira   Nice idea. But what did Zak think of that?

Miss Cherry   Oh, he was fine about it. He's such a sweetie.

Indira   And what about all the kids here? What do you lot think about going to your teacher's wedding?
Big cheer from the children.

Indira   They all seem pretty pleased about it.

Miss Cherry   Especially Sunita and Cleo. You see, they're going to be my bridesmaids.
Sunita and Cleo step forward. They are both wearing bridesmaids' dresses.

Scene 1

Indira And here are the two bridesmaids, Sunita Gohill and Cleo Hart.

Sunita looks shy but Cleo smiles and waves to the camera like a princess.

Indira Sunita, Cleo. Tell us how you got to be picked to be bridesmaids.

Cleo Well, lots of us wanted to be bridesmaids. So Miss Cherry asked us all to put our names into a hat.

Sunita And she closed her eyes and picked out two names.

Cleo Me and Sunita!

Indira How wonderful! Anyway, everything was set for the big day until, with just three days to go, you hit a bit of a problem, didn't you?

Miss Cherry We certainly did.

Indira Go on.

Miss Cherry *(Wiping away a tear)* We're not sure if Zak will get here in time for the wedding.

Scene 1

Indira Perhaps you could explain to our viewers exactly why he couldn't be here this morning?

Miss Cherry He's stranded on an island.

Indira Stranded on an island? Has he been shipwrecked?

Miss Cherry Not exactly. You see, he went to visit a small island school. And while he was there, he had an accident.

Indira Poor Zak.

Cleo Silly Zak, more like. He was dancing on a table and it broke.

Miss Cherry He was trying to explain something to the children in a dramatic way and he got a bit carried away.

Scene 1

Cleo I bet he looked funny when he crashed to the floor. *(Miming the accident herself)* Crash!

Indira What happened next, Rosie?

Miss Cherry They rushed him into the island's hospital for x-rays. But then the doctor said his leg was badly broken and he wasn't allowed to make the journey back to the mainland until next week. Poor Zak, he was so upset.

Indira And what about you? How did you feel when you heard that the wedding had to be cancelled?

Miss Cherry It was like my whole world had fallen apart. But most of all I just felt sorry for Zak. After all, there was nothing we could do.

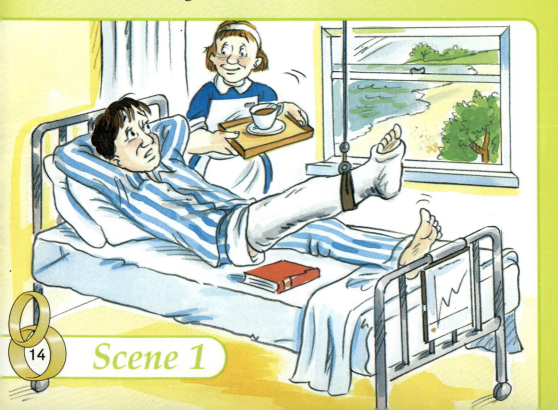

Scene 1

Indira Or that's what you all thought here at Story Street Primary School. The whole school was cast into deep gloom over the news of Zak Pieman's accident. But there was one young man who was determined that the big occasion was not going to be spoiled. Step forward, Mouse Macdonald.

Mouse comes forward and stands next to Indira.

Indira You had an idea, didn't you, Mouse?

Mouse I did.

Indira Tell us more.

Mouse I was in assembly and Mrs Turner was telling us all about Zak and how he fell off that table and broke his leg, and I just thought, well, there's got to be a way we can rescue him from that island. Like, if we could just get a helicopter to him.

Scene 1

Scene 1

Indira Sounds a bit of a tall order to me.

Mouse And that's when I thought of contacting 'Make Your Dreams Come True.'

Indira Good move!

Mouse I knew time was tight. But I asked my friend Ben to e-mail you.

Indira Smart thinking. Because as soon as we received Ben's e-mail, the 'Make Your Dreams Come True' team sprang into action. We hired a helicopter to rescue Zak from the hospital and rush him here for the wedding. Yes, even as we speak, Zak Pieman is being flown towards a reunion with Rosie. We weren't sure if he would make it in time, but any minute now the helicopter should be landing in the playground. So … what do you think of that, kids?
Big cheer from the children.

Indira The only thing is … we haven't told Zak!

Miss Cherry *(Holding her hands in front of her mouth in shock)* You mean the wedding is definitely going ahead and you haven't told him?

Indira Well, we thought we'd surprise him – though he may have recognised my co-presenter Luke Leppard, who is in the helicopter with him.

Scene 1

Miss Cherry Poor Zak! However will he cope? It will be such a shock.
Suddenly everyone is quiet. The sound of a police siren is heard in the distance.

Cleo Listen!
The siren gets louder as the police van turns into Story Street and screeches to a halt.

Police Officer *(Shouting)* Clear the playground please, folks – everyone into the tent!

Mrs Turner What's going on?!

Director *(Shouting)* OK, everyone. I want all the guests to get into their seats in the tent. As soon as you're ready, we'll open the helicopter doors.

Indira Follow me to the marquee everyone and we'll get ready to welcome the groom. I just can't wait to see his face …
Exit Miss Cherry, Mrs Turner, Sunita, Cleo, Jojo, Mouse and Sam. The helicopter noise gets much louder as it comes in to land.

Scene 1

Scene 1

Scene 2

A few minutes later, on the school playing field. In the background is the marquee. Indira, the Director and the TV crew stand waiting. A small crowd of children has gathered, including Sunita, Cleo and Donut. Others are emerging from the tent.

Director Well done, everybody, that was very quick. Now let's bring on the groom. *(Shouts)* Open up the doors! *Members of the film crew rush off. A few seconds later Zak enters being pushed in his wheelchair by members of the film crew. He has changed into his wedding suit in the helicopter. His leg is in plaster and he looks very confused.*

Zak What's going on? This isn't a hospital. Why, I'm in Wellbridge, at Story Street! I don't get this.

Zak suddenly catches sight of Rosie, who is running towards him in her wedding dress.

Zak Rosie? Rosie – you look fantastic!

Miss Cherry Zak! You're just in time for the wedding!

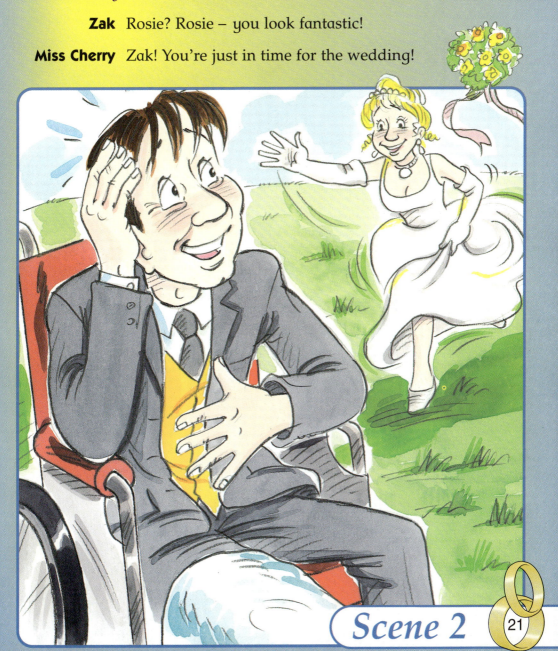

Scene 2

Scene 2

Miss Cherry throws her arms around Zak and the crew from the helicopter move towards them. TV presenter Luke Leppard steps forward and looks directly at one of the cameras.

Luke Ladies and gentlemen, this is Luke Leppard here of 'Make Your Dreams Come True.' I am joining my co-presenter Indira Das to bring you this week's brilliant suprise, live from Wellbridge. I've travelled by helicopter with Zak Pieman to reunite him with Rosie – just in time for the wedding they thought they had cancelled. Isn't it wonderful? Once again we have … **(He turns towards the crowd)**

The crowd *(Shouting)* … made your dreams come true!

Zak *(To Luke)* I thought I recognised you!

Luke Now Zak, are you ready for that wedding?

Zak No … I mean … I'm not sure. I thought it was cancelled.

Luke Don't worry. You're as ready as you ever will be.

Zak But my best man isn't here. I phoned him to say it was all off.

Luke Then you'll just have to make do with me as your best man.

Zak Have you got the ring?

Scene 2

Luke Good point. A ring. Has anyone got a ring we could use for the wedding?

Murmuring from the crowd. Cleo steps forward, waving her finger.

Cleo I've got a diamond ring. Miss Cherry can have it as her wedding ring.

Donut Don't be silly – you got that out of a Christmas cracker.

Cleo So? It's still beautiful.

Donut But people are supposed to have gold rings at weddings, not shiny plastic ones.

Scene 2

Zak Nonsense. As long as there's a ring for me to give the bride, we can be married. Anyway, it's not the metal of the ring that counts, it's the precious thoughts in my heart.

Sunita That's so sweet.

Donut Yuk!

Cleo Well, I think it's a beautiful ring and it will make Miss Cherry look like a princess.

Director Cut!

The film crew stop filming.

Scene 2

Luke What do you think, boss?

Director It is very bright and shiny. Never mind, I expect we might be able to lose it in the edit. And a ring's a ring.

Luke Let's get this wedding started.

Director First of all, we'll have to get Zak into the marquee. Who's going to push his chair?

Sunita I'd like to.

Cleo We're bridesmaids. We're supposed to help Miss Cherry.

Sunita But Miss Cherry doesn't need help and Zak does.

Director Nice idea, girls. That would make a great first shot. Two bridesmaids wheeling in the groom. Unusual but I like it. Let's go for it. And … action!
The film crew start to film again. Sunita and Cleo push Zak very quickly in his wheelchair towards the marquee. Zak looks anxious.

Zak *(Frightened)* Steady on, girls. I've already had one accident. To the left a bit. Look out!

Director Cut! Cut! We're not chariot racing now, girls.

Cleo We thought he would be in a hurry to get married.

Zak Not that much of a hurry!

Scene 2

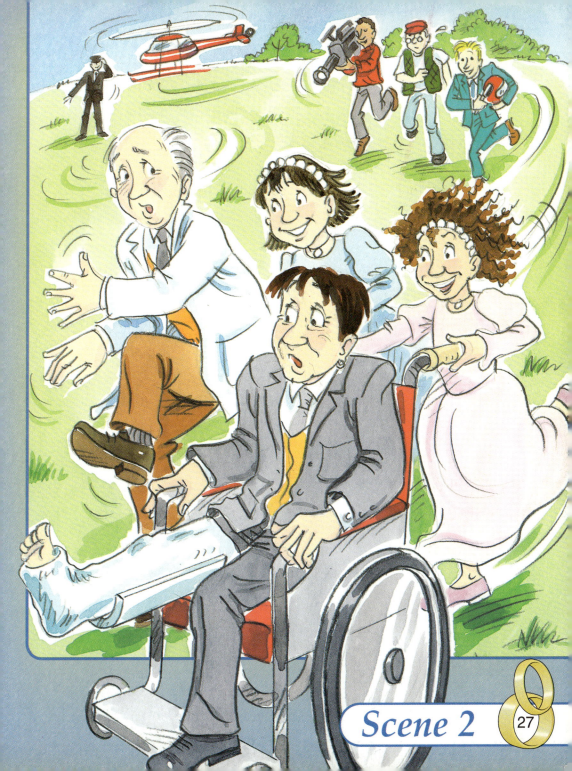

Scene 2

Director Can we take that one more time? Go back and start again, only this time try to be slower and more graceful. You're meant to be bridesmaids, not racing drivers.

Sunita We'll try. Sorry, Zak.

Sunita and Cleo reverse and start again, this time much more slowly. As they pass the camera, Cleo waves to it.

Scene 2

Scene 3

Half an hour later. In front of the marquee. The wedding group is gathered for a photograph with Miss Cherry, Zak, Luke, Sunita and Cleo at the centre. The Director and film crew are organising everyone. There is a crowd of spectators, including Mr and Mrs Green.

Director That's it. Everyone look this way and smile. Perfect.

Luke *(To the camera)* A perfect ending to a perfect day here in Wellbridge. We've all had a marvellous time.
(To Mr Green) How would you sum up the day, sir?

Mr Green Oh, it's been a grand day, all right. Almost perfect, but not quite.

Luke Why's that?

Mr Green I'm still looking for that cup of tea, you know. I haven't managed to find one yet.

Mrs Green Oh, Eric, you are terrible. Never happy unless there's something to complain about.

Sam Don't worry, Mr Green. Follow me. I'll take you over to the refreshments. There's champagne as well as tea!

Mrs Green You do that, Sam, and we'll get you an ice cream.

Mr Green Will we?

Mrs Green Of course we will. Come on, Sam.

Exit Sam with Mr and Mrs Green.

Luke And what about the happy couple? Have you enjoyed your big surprise?

Scene 3

Mrs Pieman Oh Luke, it's been wonderful. I can't tell you how happy I am that we've been able to have the wedding today with all our friends from Story Street. I'm so glad you were able to rescue Zak.

Indira How about you, Zak?

Zak What can I say, Luke? It's been an amazing week. A bit like a rollercoaster ride. Yesterday I was down in the dumps, all my wedding plans in tatters. Today – well, it's been the best day of my life.

Luke *(To Mrs Turner)* Mrs Turner, you must be very happy too.

Scene 3

Mrs Turner It's been a tremendous day for everyone connected with our school. The children, the teachers, our ex-pupils, they've all been part of a very special occasion. We said we wanted a party but thanks to you it's been a really special one – the biggest party in the universe!

Luke That's what we like to hear. And with those happy words it's time to leave Wellbridge. Remember, we'll be back next week at the same time when once again we'll …

Crowd *(Loud)* … Make Your Dreams Come True!

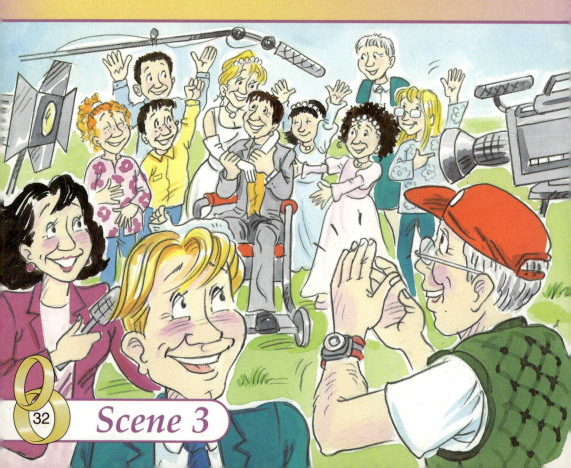

Scene 3